Autism

Sudipta Bardhan-Quallen

KIDHAVEN PRESS

An imprint of Thomson Gale, a part of The Thomson Corporation

THOMSON

━━━━✦━━━━™

GALE

Detroit • New York • San Francisco • San Diego • New Haven, Conn. • Waterville, Maine • London • Munich

THOMSON
GALE ™

Picture Credits:

Cover photo: © Images.com/CORBIS
Henny Allis/Photo Researchers, Inc., 25
AP/Wide World Photos, 18, 19, 24, 27, 28, 30, 36
© Bernard Bisson/SYGMA/CORBIS, 7, 13
Oscar Burriel/Photo Researchers, Inc., 5
© Reg Charity/CORBIS, 22
Getty Images, 9

© Images.com/CORBIS, 15 (background)
© Michael Macor/San Francisco Chronicle/CORBIS, 33
Brandy Noon, 15 (chart text)
Photos.com, 23
© Jeffrey L. Rotman/CORBIS, 38
© Andres Stapff/Reuters/CORBIS, 10
Time Life Pictures/Getty Images, 16, 35

For more information, contact
KidHaven Press
27500 Drake Rd.
Farmington Hills, MI 48331-3535
Or you can visit our Internet site at http://www.gale.com

LIBRARY OF CONGRESS CATALOGING-IN-PUBLICATION DATA

Bardhan-Quallen, Sudipta.
  Autism / by Sudipta Bardhan-Quallen.
    p. cm. — (Understanding diseases and disorders)
  Includes bibliographical references and index.
Contents: What is autism?—What are the symptoms of autism?—Treating autism—Living with autism.
  ISBN 0-7377-2167-7 (hardcover : alk. paper)
  1. Autism—Juvenile literature. I. Title. II. Series.
  RC553.A88B365 2005
  616.85'882—dc22

                                                    2004021343

Printed in the United States of America

Contents

Chapter One

What Is Autism?

When the brain works correctly, it controls how a person's body functions. It also controls how a person communicates and interacts with other people. In a person with autism (or an autistic), however, the brain does not develop properly. People with autism have difficulty talking to others, getting along with others, and performing everyday tasks.

Many people have autism. Experts estimate that out of every 1,000 people, between 2 and 6 have the **disorder**. Approximately 1.5 million people with autism live in the United States alone. In addition, autism is increasing in part because doctors are more aware of the symptoms and can diagnose it better. A 2002 study in just one state, California, found that between 1987 and 1998, the number of autism cases increased by 273 percent. In Missouri, autism cases have increased 850 percent since 1991. In Rhode Island, autism cases increased by 115 percent between 1994 and 2002. The Autism Society of America estimates that every day 50 American children are diagnosed with some form of

A girl wears tape over her mouth and plugs her ears to represent how isolated people with autism can feel.

autism. Experts believe there may be more than 4 million cases of autism in the United States within a decade.

Autism was not identified as a specific disorder until 1943. In that year, Leo Kanner published a study that discussed eleven children he had been working with since 1938. These children did not seem to be interested in other people, socially or emotionally. They did not cuddle or make eye contact, and they had trouble learning to speak. Many did not speak at

Autistic children like this girl often withdraw and cut themselves off from other people.

all. On the other hand, they showed a lot of interest in unusual things around them. For example, upon entering a room, one child ignored people completely and instead set as many objects spinning as he could. Another child turned the lights on and off upon entering any room. Kanner felt that these children were not emotionally disturbed or mentally retarded. Nor did he think they were just slow learners. Kanner diagnosed these children with early infantile autism. His work with these autistic children helped spark a medical interest in this condition.

The word *autism* comes from the Greek word meaning "self." People with autism withdraw into themselves. As Kanner saw, they cut themselves off from other human or emotional contact. In the 1940s, however, no one knew what caused autism or how to treat it.

What Causes Autism?

In the 1950s and 1960s, soon after Kanner discovered autism as a disorder, doctors believed incorrectly that children developed autism because they were raised by uncaring parents. For years parents were blamed for their children's autism. In 1964, however, Bernard Rimland published a study that proved that autism was a condition that children were born with, rather than a result of the way they were raised.

Later, when brain scans and similar tests were available, scientists learned that the shape and structure of the brains of autistics were different than those of people without autism. Unfortunately, scientists do not yet know why these differences occur.

Both Rimland and other scientists seemed to prove that autism might be a **genetic**, or inherited, disorder. Genes are responsible for many parts of life. They control characteristics such as eye color and straight or curly hair. Genes also can be responsible for diseases and disorders such as breast cancer and diabetes.

Scientists have not yet found genes that cause autism, but there is a lot of proof that people may inherit the disorder. In 2004, Joseph Buxbaum and other researchers in New York City studied 411 families with a history of autism. They found at least one **defective** gene, called **SLC25A12**, in all of them. The researchers realized that a problem with this one gene would not be enough to cause autism. Instead, the gene increased the risk that a person might develop the disorder. Scientists are working on identifying more genes that are linked to autism.

Other Factors Involved in Autism

Autism also may be linked to problems during pregnancy. Scientists already know that **birth defects** can occur when pregnant women experience stress, develop certain illnesses, or are exposed to certain chemicals. Throughout pregnancy, the child's brain is developing in complex ways. Anything that interferes with proper brain development may lead to autism.

These twins, who were born with autism, may have inherited the disorder from a parent.

Many different studies have linked autism with pregnancy. A 2002 Swedish study seemed to show that women who smoke during pregnancy are 40 percent more likely to have autistic children. Another 2002 study reported that women who experience heavy stress during their pregnancy have a greater risk of having an autistic child. David Beversdorf, who studied stress and autism, says, "There is now evidence through this study that autism is also linked to **external factors**, such as prenatal stress."[1]

What Is Autism? 9

Researchers continue to try to understand the causes of autism. They now believe that autism is probably caused by both defective genes and other factors. As David Amaral explains, "We know that it's a very complicated genetic disorder, but it's also probably true that genes are not the entire answer. It's most likely a combination of genetic[s] . . . and an environmental disorder."[2]

Boys are more likely to be autistic than girls. In this photo of students at a school for autistics, the boys clearly outnumber the girls.

Who Has Autism?

Interestingly, boys are four times more likely to be autistic than girls are. Scientists believe that this difference results from the genetic aspect of the disorder. Somehow boys are more at risk than girls are for inheriting the defects that result in autism.

Autism is found throughout the world. There does not appear to be any link between autism and race, social status, or wealth. Therefore the growing problem of autism is a concern for everyone.

Chapter Two

What Are the Symptoms of Autism?

Autism is a **spectrum disorder**. People who are autistic may experience a wide range of symptoms. The symptoms may be mild to severe, and two people may have completely different experiences. Symptoms common to autistic people include making little or no eye contact; repeating words or phrases instead of responding appropriately; spinning objects; insisting on routine; laughing or crying for reasons that are not clear to others; wanting to be alone or having difficulty mixing with others; being oversensitive or undersensitive to pain; not responding when others talk; having difficulty expressing needs with words; throwing tantrums;

being apparently fearless of danger; and avoiding close contact such as cuddling.

How Is Autism Diagnosed?

Marcel Augier is a boy in Cleveland, Ohio, with autism. When he was two years old, his parents noticed that his behavior seemed strange. Although he had just begun to talk, Marcel suddenly stopped

An autistic child throws a tantrum, one of the common behaviors in autism.

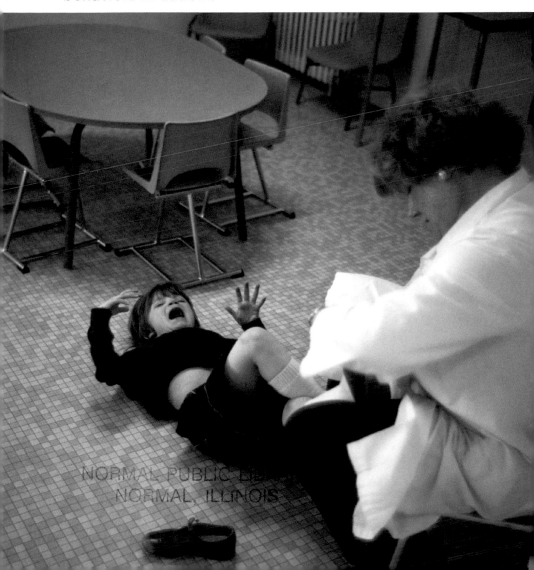

talking and responding to his parents. Other strange behaviors soon followed. Marcel would shake his hands in front of his face; he stopped making eye contact with people; and he did not react to presents or family outings.

Marcel was diagnosed with autism. He could not tell anyone when he was hungry or tired. He could not communicate to his parents when he was scared. Marcel would become frustrated and throw tantrums.

Marcel's diagnosis is typical of many cases of autism. Most can be diagnosed before three years of age. According to the National Institute of Child Health and Human Development's Autism Facts, a child should see a doctor immediately if he or she does not babble, coo, or gesture by pointing, waving, or grasping by age one. A child is also at risk who does not say single words by sixteen months of age or two-word phrases (that are not repetitions of others' speech) by age two or who loses any language or social skills (such as ceasing to babble) at any age. These behaviors are common red flags for autism.

Autistic People Are "Mind Blind"

Often, autistics are "**mind blind**." This means that they think that what is in their mind is the same as what is in everyone else's mind. They do not understand that other people may have different viewpoints or opinions. Furthermore, they do not

Common Traits of People with Autism

Cannot imitate others

Do not like change

Unafraid of danger

Do things over and over

Throw tantrums

Have few social skills

Cannot communicate needs

Avoid making eye contact

Have poor language skills

Do not like cuddling

May be "mind blind"

understand that other people might lie, hide something, or even try to control situations.

One example of mind blindness is seen in fourteen-year-old Andrew Bacalao, who has autism. Andrew excels at video games and jigsaw puzzles and has an incredible memory for phone numbers. When it comes to being with people, however, Andrew has problems. When Andrew saw a guest wearing a jacket in the house, he told her, "I'm going to unbutton your outfit."[3] Andrew meant that he would take the guest's jacket and did not understand that his words could be taken wrong.

Mind blindness extends to actions as well as words. In Andrew's case, he has trouble understanding that actions might mean something different to others than they do to him. During an interview with *Newsweek* magazine, Andrew was asked to look at the journalist. He responded by continuing to play a video game and then running outside to bang on the windows. Those actions seemed normal

An autistic boy mimics the actions of his teacher. Such therapy helps him to better understand human body language.

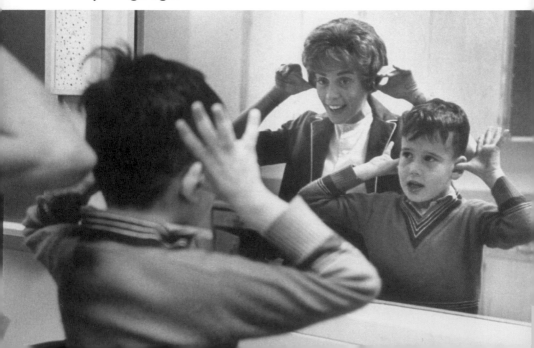

and appropriate to Andrew, even though to others, they seemed out of place.

Child psychologist Andrew Meltzoff believes that the mind blindness seen in autism occurs because autistic children do not imitate others around them. For example, if an adult does something such as make faces or pound blocks in front of a healthy eighteen-month-old child, the child will probably imitate the actions. This imitation is an important learning tool. This is what helps children learn to mouth their first words and understand body language. An autistic child, however, does not imitate others and therefore does not learn how to read other people's expressions or body language.

High-Functioning Autism

Not all autistics experience mind blindness as Andrew does. Because autism is a spectrum disorder, some autistics experience only minor symptoms. Therefore, mind blindness is not always debilitating. Many people with autism are able to learn to figure out at least some of the emotions of others, although with a great amount of struggle.

Some autistics, in fact, have average or above-average intelligence and can function in school or in the workplace with little help from others. These people are said to have high-functioning autism.

Temple Grandin is an example of a person with high-functioning autism. When Grandin was two and a half years old, she began to show symptoms

High-functioning autistics like Temple Grandin are able to maintain successful careers despite the challenges they face.

of autism. She did not talk and threw tantrums. Loud noises hurt her ears. Therefore, as Grandin explains, "I would shut out the [noise] by rocking or staring at sand dribbling through my fingers."[4]

Grandin went to school, but she had a difficult time making friends. She could not relate to the emotions of her peers. "Even today," Grandin says, "personal relationships are something I don't really understand."[5]

Grandin is able to function in society. In fact, she is an assistant professor of animal sciences at Colorado State University. Still, she realizes that the way she views the world is very different from the way other people do. Grandin explains that she translates words into pictures in order to under-stand them. The words themselves carry no mean-ing for her. As she explains it, "Autistics have trouble learning things that cannot be thought about in pic-tures. The easiest words for an autistic child to learn are nouns because they relate directly to pictures. Spatial words such as *over* and *under* had no meaning for me until I had a visual image to fix them in my memory." [6]

Special Skills

Although autistics often have trouble mixing in soci-ety, their symptoms do not always keep them from leading a full life. In fact, sometimes the skills that autistics have can be put to good use. For example, some people with autism have almost geniuslike memory skills, math ability, or puzzle-decoding

Concert pianist Leslie Lemke is an example of an autistic person with geniuslike skills.

expertise. As Geraldine Dawson, professor of psychology and director of the autism project at the University of Washington, explains, "Some children (with autism) have islets of . . . exceptional ability. . . . It's similar to a person who is blind who has more acute hearing or ability to use touch. If you're not using certain areas of the brain involved with language and people, other areas having to do with objects, space, and numbers are exercised."[7]

By recognizing the skills of a person with autism, the rest of society can learn to accept him or her into normal life. Furthermore, many treatment options often can improve an autistic's symptoms.

Chapter Three

Treating Autism

There is no cure for autism. But doctors do know of some therapies and medications that seem to improve the lives of autistic people. Because each autistic has different symptoms, doctors cannot guarantee that any one treatment will work for every patient.

A Range of Treatments

The treatments for autism include dietary changes, medications for certain symptoms, and intensive teaching to change behavior. Some treatments seem to make a difference to some autistic people.

People with autism sometimes follow strict diets because they cannot tolerate or are allergic to certain foods. When they eat those foods, their bodies react badly. Avoiding these foods can prevent certain behavioral and medical problems such as confusion, hyperactivity, stomach problems, and fatigue.

A study in the United Kingdom found that some autistic children have difficulty digesting foods that contain certain proteins such as gluten or casein. Gluten is found in wheat, oats, and rye. Casein is

Some autistic children have trouble digesting foods containing certain proteins such as casein, found in dairy products.

found in dairy products. Sometimes when foods containing gluten and casein are removed from an autistic's diet, the symptoms improve.

Other studies have shown that autistic people may have imbalances in vitamins and minerals. In particular,

Many autistic children cannot digest gluten, a protein found in grains.

several studies suggest that increasing vitamin B in an autistic's diet can improve symptoms. Vitamin B plays an important role in creating proteins that are needed by the brain. Giving vitamin B to people with autism appears to decrease behavioral problems, improve their ability to make eye contact, and help them pay better attention.

Medications also are being used to treat the symptoms of autism. Drugs that are used to treat anxiety, **obsessive-compulsive disorder**, hyperactivity, or aggression in people without autism, for example, are now sometimes prescribed to autistic people. The drugs must be carefully monitored by doctors, however, as they have side effects and sometimes cause more serious problems than those they are used to treat.

Applied Behavior Analysis

Although diet and medications are becoming more common ways to treat some symptoms of autism,

Using applied behavior analysis, a therapist plays with a young autistic boy to help improve his social skills.

most experts suggest that autistics learn **behavior modification**. The most widely accepted way to treat autistic people is an approach called **applied behavior analysis**, or **ABA**. ABA is a program in which autistics work one-on-one with a teacher to change any destructive or unacceptable behaviors into more socially acceptable ones. As developmental pediatrician Cecilia McCarton explains,

> When your [autistic] child demonstrates an appropriate behavior, he gets rewarded. When he

demonstrates an inappropriate behavior, he doesn't get punished; instead, the behavior is ignored, or he's taught to do something more appropriate. Recent studies show that with intensive one-on-one ABA therapy between a therapist and a child, 40 hours a week, children can actually both regain skills they lost and continue learning.[8]

Karen Siff's son, Jake, is one of McCarton's patients. Jake was diagnosed with autism after his second birthday. McCarton suggested that Jake undergo forty hours a week of ABA, but she did not guarantee that the therapy would change Jake's behavior.

Using an ABA program, a mother helps her autistic son work on his communication skills.

Siff herself became one of Jake's therapists. Part of each session was to give Jake simple instructions such as "sit down," "stand up," or "turn around." Each instruction was repeated 30 times. Siff recorded Jake's response to each instruction. If Jake succeeded in the task, he was rewarded with candy, chocolate chips, hugs, and tickles. Says Siff, "It took a total of 150 trials over three weeks to teach Jake to sit down, 180 trials over three weeks to teach Jake to stand up, and 2,100 trials over 10 weeks to teach Jake to look at us when we called his name."[9] In addition, after nearly 9 months of ABA therapy, Jake was able to tell his mother that he loved her, an emotion that many autistics are unable to communicate.

Jake can now do many things that other children his age can do. He is able to use the toilet by himself and make friends with other children. He attends a regular preschool with trained therapists shadowing him. Says Siff, "I know that my son still needs help. . . . [But] Franklin [Jake's father] and I are committed to continue with his therapy. We'll do it until we are sure that Jake can make it on his own."[10]

Rapid Prompting Method

Other ways to treat autism are being tested. One way that seems to succeed with some autistic children was developed by Soma Mukhopadhyay. Mukhopadhyay's son, Tito, is from India and has severe autism. He is almost **mute** and has little control over his body. Tito's doctors told his mother

A woman spells out words on paper as her autistic son holds on to her hand.

that her son would never be able to learn. Mukhopadhyay did not accept the doctors' diagnosis. She gave up her career to stay home with Tito and teach him.

Mukhopadhyay noticed that Tito often stared at calendars, so she tried to teach him numbers and letters. Tito would not hold a pencil, so Mukhopadhyay attached a pencil to his finger with a rubber band. Tito first learned to draw lines. Eventually he could write words. Mukhopadhyay must spend a great deal of her time keeping Tito busy. She speaks to him constantly to keep his mind on track. She teaches Tito everything from math to music to Shakespeare.

Because Tito can write, he is able to talk about what it is like to be autistic. For example, when asked what he thinks people think of autism, Tito writes, "That they don't have any understanding."[11]

Mukhopadhyay brought her son to California to share her teaching methods with other parents of autistic children. Tito's doctor in the United States, Mike Merzenich with the University of California at San Francisco, believes Tito is an authentic autistic who is also miraculous. He thinks Tito is an example of what is possible for autistic people. He

An autistic boy responds with a smile as a butterfly lands on his nose during an ABA therapy session.

says, "I think there could be thousands, maybe tens of thousands of Titos out there." [12]

Working with a foundation called Cure Autism Now (CAN), Mukhopadhyay teaches a small group of autistic children in Los Angeles. One of her students is Dov Shestack. Before Mukhopadhyay's classes, Dov made only garbled noises and he could not control his movements. He could not even tie his own shoes. His parents and teachers had no idea if anything they said or did got through to Dov.

Remarkable Changes

After a year of classes with Mukhopadhyay, Dov writes complete sentences and complex thoughts. Dov has communicated to his parents that he enjoys religion, history, and math. He also has communicated that in all the years that people thought he was lost in his own world, he was actually listening to—and learning from—everything around him. He is a much happier child now, because, as he writes, "I can tell others my feelings." [13]

Mukhopadhyay has worked individually with more than seventy autistic children in the United States. The parents of these children say that the changes in their children, as in Dov, have been remarkable. Mukhopadhyay's methods have not yet been studied scientifically, but Merzenich believes that it is a promising therapy for autism. He says, "I think it's almost certain that this method can be used with many, many autistic children, and the initial indication

This father sends his autistic sons to a learning center where the teachers are trained to meet the children's specific needs.

from the studies in Los Angeles is that it might apply even to the substantial majority of these children."[14]

Who Will Pay for Treatments?

As seen in the cases of Jake, Tito, and Dov, the quality of an autistic person's life is greatly affected by treatment. Because there is no cure for autism, treatment is lifelong. Programs such as ABA or the rapid prompting method require near-constant attention and are very expensive to maintain.

In the United States, schools are required to provide free and appropriate schooling for autistic children. Unfortunately, there is no standard for what is considered "appropriate." For example, Karen and Dan McGuire, who live in Chicago, have an autistic son, Danny. Their school district has offered the McGuires access to a school for Danny that is over an hour away from their home. "This is putting a three-year-old, nonverbal child on a bus—who'd never been—never done that before. I couldn't do it,"[15] explains Karen. Instead, the McGuires pay for ABA therapy on their own. Yearly care costs more than $60,000, which is more than Dan makes as a police officer. Still, many families believe the treatment is well worth the cost and find creative ways to pay for it. As Siff says, "The son we thought we'd lost has come back to us. We don't want to lose him again."[16]

Chapter Four

Living with Autism

Even with treatment, it can be difficult to live with autism—for the autistic as well as for his or her family. In some cases, a person with autism must be cared for twenty-four hours a day, by family or by medical professionals. Noah Greenfeld is one such person. Noah cannot speak, dress himself, or use the bathroom without help. He has temper tantrums and violent outbursts. Growing up, Noah's brother, Karl Taro Greenfeld, remembers that Noah's autism affected every part of their family's life. Says Karl, "Noah's condition dictated what we ate and when we slept and to a great degree how we lived. We never had fancy furniture because he chewed on the couch cushions and spit on the carpets. He would pull apart anything more complicated than a pencil."[17] Because Noah's autism is so severe, he has lived in institutions for autistic people since he was eighteen years old.

Stress on Families

In many cases, autistics do not have symptoms serious enough to need professional medical care. Nevertheless they do need almost constant supervision. In these cases, a lot of stress is placed on the

Living with autism presents many challenges. A simple task like tying shoes is frustrating for some autistics.

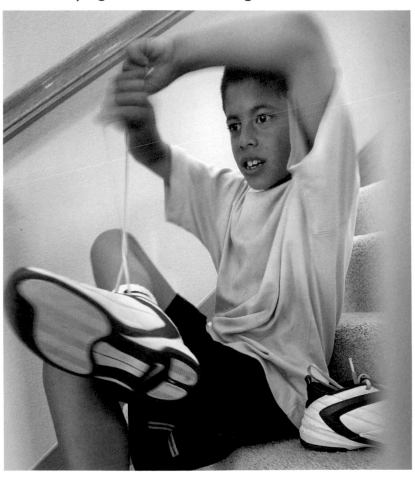

autistic person's family. For example, Brandon Garrison has autism. His parents and his sister, Melissa, have had to make many adjustments to care for Brandon properly.

Brandon has needed constant care since he was a baby. This has made it difficult for his parents to give attention to any other family member or for the family to find time to do anything else but care for Brandon. As Melissa recalls, "I didn't get why there wasn't time to go out on the weekends anymore. There wasn't time to do this. There wasn't time to do that. Because everybody was so busy with Brandon."[18]

Melissa and her parents have learned to communicate with Brandon in ways that make sense to him. Melissa says,

> You have different voices, for different situations—different inflections that you have to use, so he knows what you are talking about. If he is having a tantrum . . . you can't go in there like you would to a typically developing sibling and say, "You stop that, or you are going to your room." You say, "Brandon, you know, calm down. Why are you doing this? It's time to stop."[19]

Melissa, like many siblings of autistics, is protective of Brandon. "I've got to watch out, be careful with him,"[20] she explains. To deal with the stress of

This woman outfits her autistic son with protective gear to keep him from harming himself. Many autistics need constant supervision.

having an autistic brother, Melissa attends a support group called Sibshop. Sibshop meetings are places for children similar to Melissa who have relatives with autism. At meetings they can talk about their experiences among their peers. This helps manage the stress of caring for a family member with autism.

Melissa realizes that taking care of Brandon is a lifelong commitment. She has already begun to plan for a time when her parents will not be taking care of him. She explains, "I know that if I ever get married, I am going to make sure that my husband is OK with [taking care of Brandon]. I know that if the time does come when Brandon needs somewhere else to go, then it's gonna be me. And I am OK with that. I am ready to accept that. I want that." [21]

A Place for Autistics in Society

Even though their symptoms create many issues for autistics, they can be a part of society. No matter where on the autistic spectrum a person falls, there are jobs that he or she can perform. As Grandin writes,

> A person with . . . autism has to compensate for poor social skills by making themselves so good in a specialized field that people will be willing to "buy" their skill even though social

All autistics can make positive contributions to society. Many are successful in jobs that entail repetitive work.

skills are poor. . . . You need to learn a few social survival skills, but you will make friends at work by sharing your shared interest with the other people who work in your specialty.[22]

Grandin suggests a variety of jobs for autistics with different skills. For example, high-functioning autistics who think in pictures are often very successful in computer programming, drafting, veterinary medicine, and animal training or as laboratory technicians, mechanics, and maintenance workers. For other autistics who are good at math, music, or facts but do not think visually, Grandin suggests careers in accounting, engineering, inventory control, and mathematics or as bank tellers, filing clerks, or copy editors. These jobs require good long-term memory skills, which autistics often have.

Grandin feels that even autistics who have poor language skills or who do not communicate by talking can perform useful jobs. She suggests that these people be given jobs with repetitive actions, such as reshelving library books, running photocopies at a copy shop, restocking shelves at stores, sorting at recycling plants, or loading trucks.

Planning for the Future

Living with autism is a challenge, but one that is becoming more manageable with every passing day. Autistics now have a voice in society and can speak for themselves to help others understand

A trainer introduces an autistic child to a dolphin.
Animal therapy is one of many new treatments
available to autistics.

their disease. Grandin, Mukhopadhyay, and Dov
have already done this. So too has Wendy Lawson,
a poet and a writer who has autism. Lawson writes,

> Autism is: being present in this world,
> But not entirely of it.
> I am one step removed and curled,
> The switch just doesn't click. [23]

These words from autistic people make autism less
mysterious for doctors, scientists, and the rest of
society.

With additional research and treatment options, there is hope for many autistics to live more normal lives. There is also hope for the rest of society to better understand the autistic experience. Says Dr. Howard Buten, founder of an autism treatment center outside Paris, "Accepting the autisms of the autistic—being able to appreciate them, even—demands certain human sensibilities that are not given to everyone."[24] The goal for the future is to have more and more people making strides toward understanding autism.

Notes

Chapter 1: What Is Autism?
1. Quoted in *Science Daily,* "Major Stress During Pregnancy Linked to Autism," November 28, 2001. www.sciencedaily.com.
2. Quoted in Ulysses Torassa, "Autism Rate Doubles Among State's Kids," *San Francisco Chronicle,* May 14, 2003. http://sfgate.com/chronicle.

Chapter 2: What Are the Symptoms of Autism?
3. Quoted in Geoffrey Cowley, "Girls, Boys and Autism," *Newsweek,* September 4, 2003. www.msnbc.msn.com.
4. Temple Grandin, "Myself," *Time,* May 6, 2002. www.time.com.
5. Grandin, "Myself."
6. Grandin, "Myself."
7. Quoted in Carol Smith, "Autism on the Rise, Along with Concerns over Treatment," *Seattle Post-Intelligencer,* November 15, 1999. http://seattle pi.nwsource.com.

Chapter 3: Treating Autism

8. Quoted in Karen Siff, "Finding Jake: A Mother's Story," *Nightline,* March 14, 2001. www.abcnews.com.

9. Siff, "Finding Jake."

10. Siff, "Finding Jake."

11. Quoted in Vicki Mabrey, "Breaking the Silence," *60 Minutes II,* July 16, 2003. www.cbsnews.com.

12. Quoted in Mabrey, "Breaking the Silence."

13. Quoted in Mabrey, "Breaking the Silence."

14. Quoted in Mabrey, "Breaking the Silence."

15. Quoted in Dawn Fratangelo, "One Family's Struggle with Autism," *NBC Nightly News with Tom Brokaw,* April 19, 2004. www.msnbc.msn.com.

16. Siff, "Finding Jake."

Chapter 4: Living with Autism

17. Karl Taro Greenfeld, "My Brother," *Time,* May 6, 2002. www.time.com.

18. Quoted in Bob Brown, "Sisterly Love," *ABC News,* May 22, 2004. www.abcnews.com.

19. Quoted in Brown, "Sisterly Love."

20. Quoted in Brown, "Sisterly Love."

21. Quoted in Brown, "Sisterly Love."

22. Temple Grandin, "Choosing the Right Job for People with Autism or Asperger's Syndrome," Center for the Study of Autism, November 1999. www.autism.org.

23. Wendy Lawson, "Wendy Lawson's Home Page," http://mugsy.org/wendy/index2.htm.

24. Quoted in John Langone, "Into the Mind of the Autistic," *New York Times,* August 10, 2004. www.nytimes.com.

Glossary

applied behavior analysis (ABA): The most widely accepted way to treat autistic people in which autistics work one-on-one with a teacher to change any destructive or unacceptable behaviors into more socially acceptable ones.

behavior modification: The process through which destructive or unacceptable behaviors are changed, often through intensive teaching.

birth defects: Medical problems that affect a baby during pregnancy.

defective: Genes are defective when they do not function properly.

disorder: A medical condition.

external factors: Outside influences that affect a person's medical condition that are not related to his or her genes. External factors include the environment, stress, and chemicals.

genetic: Something that is inherited from a person's parents.

"mind blind": A term that means that an autistic person thinks that what is in his or her mind is the same as in everyone else's mind.

mute: Unable to speak or communicate verbally.

obsessive-compulsive disorder: An anxiety disorder that is characterized by the obsessive need to perform a task over and over again.

SLC25A12: A gene thought to be involved in causing autism.

spectrum disorder: A disorder in which different people can suffer a wide range of symptoms.

For Further Exploration

Books

Fiona Bleach, *Everybody Is Different: A Book for Young People Who Have Brothers or Sisters with Autism.* Shawnee Mission, KS: Autism Asperger, 2002. This book is aimed at the brothers and sisters of autistic people and helps to explain the disorder as well as offer suggestions for making family life more comfortable.

Kari Dunn Buron and Brenda Smith Myles, *When My Autism Gets Too Big! A Relaxation Book for Children with Autism Spectrum Disorders.* Shawnee Mission, KS: Autism Asperger, 2004. A book aimed at autistic children and their caregivers to help explore their feelings and experiences.

Michele Engel Edwards, *Autism.* San Diego: Lucent Books, 2001. This book discusses the definition of autism, how it may be caused, and how it can be treated.

Temple Grandin, *Thinking in Pictures: And Other Reports from My Life with Autism.* New York: Vintage Books USA, 1996. In this book, Grandin recounts her own life as an autistic and how thinking in pictures rather than in words has helped her have a full and meaningful life.

Catherine Maurice, *Let Me Hear Your Voice: A Family's Triumph over Autism.* New York: Ballantine Books, 1994. This book explores the story of a family with two autistic children and the methods they used to create a more normal life.

Web Sites

Autism Society of America (www.autism-society. org). The Autism Society of America (ASA) was founded in 1965 and now has more than twenty thousand members in nearly every state. The ASA provides education, advocates on behalf of autistics and their families, promotes public awareness campaigns, and supports autism research. Their Web site is a comprehensive source of information on autism.

Center for the Study of Autism (www.autism. org). This Web site provides autism information to parents, doctors, and researchers. The Center for the Study of Autism also conducts research on different therapies for autism and related disorders.

Cure Autism Now (CAN) (www.cureautismnow. org). Cure Autism Now (CAN) is an organization of parents, doctors, and researchers who support autism research through fund-raising for research projects and autism education. This Web site provides a wealth of information about autism and autism treatments.

Index

imitation, 17
infantile autism, early, 7
inherited disorders, 8, 10, 11
intelligence, 17

jobs, 36–37

Kanner, Leo, 6–7

language skills
  after ABA therapy, 26
  development of, 13–14
  of high-functioning autistic
    persons, 19
  jobs for those with poor, 37
  of mind blind, 17
Lawson, Wendy, 38
learning, 17, 19

McCarton, Cecilia, 24–25
McGuire, Dan, 31
McGuire, Danny, 31
McGuire, Karen, 31
medications, 23
Meltzoff, Andrew, 17
Merzenich, Mike, 28–30
mind blindness, 14–17
minerals, 23
Mukhopadhyay, Soma, 26–28, 29
Mukhopadhyay, Tito, 26–28

name, 7
Newsweek (magazine), 17

parents, as cause, 7
population, 4–6, 11
pregnancy problems, 8–9

rapid prompting method, 26–30

Rimland, Bernard, 7, 8

severe autism, 26–28, 32–33
Shestack, Dov, 29
Sibshop, 35
Siff, Jake, 25–26
Siff, Karen, 25, 26
skills
  social, 17, 36–37
  useful, 19–20, 37
SLC25A12 gene, 8
smoking, 9
spectrum disorders, 12, 17
stress
  on families, 33–35
  during pregnancy, 9
supervision, 32–34
symptoms
  common, 6–7, 12–13
  of high-functioning autism, 17–19
  increased awareness of, 4
  of mind blindness, 14–17
  to see doctor about, 14
  of severe autism, 26, 29, 32

tantrums, 14
treatment(s)
  applied behavior analysis, 24–26
  cost, 30–31
  diet, 21–23
  medications, 23
  rapid prompting method, 26–30
types
  early infantile autism, 7
  high-functioning autism, 17–19, 37
  mind blindness, 14–17
  severe autism, 26–28, 32–33

vitamins, 23

Index **47**

About the Author

Sudipta Bardhan-Quallen holds a bachelor's degree and a master's degree, both in biology, from the California Institute of Technology. Her writing interests range from nonfiction for young adults to poetry for children. She lives in New Jersey with her husband and two daughters.